THE
BEST 50

PHYLLO RECIPES

Christie Katona
Thomas Katona

BRISTOL PUBLISHING ENTERPRISES
San Leandro, California

Printed in the United States of America.

ISBN 1-55867-143-9

Cover design: Frank J. Paredes
Cover photography: John A. Benson
Food stylist: Suzanne Carreiro

ABOUT PHYLLO

If you mention phyllo, most people immediately think of baklava, that delicious honey-filled pastry that seems rich and aromatic, yet light and delicate at the same time. By most accounts, baklava originated in the court of the sultans in Istanbul between the twelfth and fifteenth centuries. The dough was a refined version of a flattened bread called yufka, a staple of Turkish nomadic tribes for centuries before the invention of baklava. It is believed that European strudel is an offshoot of the phyllo method of pastry cooking, transferred by the Turks during the invasion and occupation of what is now southeastern Europe.

Regardless of who invented it, phyllo pastry is the basis of a wonderful variety of dishes ranging from savory to sweet, the best of which are provided in this book. You will find recipes that you can use for everyday cooking as well as recipes that will impress your guests on those special occasions. Enjoy them and have fun making them at the same time. Bon apetit!

SHAPING PHYLLO

You will find it easier to work with fresh versus frozen phyllo; however, frozen phyllo is very convenient and can be stored for up to a year in the freezer if unopened. If you plan to use frozen phyllo, let it thaw in the refrigerator overnight, remove it and let it stand at room temperature for about 1 hour before working with it. Both fresh and frozen phyllo dough can usually be purchased at your local supermarket. It commonly comes in a 1-pound size with about 20 sheets per package; each sheet is about 12-x-20 inches.

Usually, the only tools you need for working with ready-made phyllo are a good pastry brush about 1½ to 2 inches wide, a sharp knife and a pair of scissors.

Your work surface should be clean, dry and out of direct sunlight or other sources of heat. The phyllo sheets, or "leaves" as they are sometime called, are very thin and can quickly dry out if exposed to air or heat. Work quickly and cover unused phyllo dough with a piece of plastic wrap topped with a damp towel until you need it. Some people use a misting spray bottle to prevent phyllo from drying out, but do not get your work surface wet or the sheets will stick to it.

If your dough is in good condition, you should be able to easily separate the phyllo leaves. If they stick together, try to gently peel them apart at the edges. If unsuccessful, all is not lost. You can generally use 2 layers which are stuck together as long as you generously butter them. If you purchased fresh phyllo from your supermarket and the sheets stick together, consider returning it for a fresher product, or getting a refund and finding a better source.

Each phyllo sheet should be brushed with just enough butter or oil to completely cover the surface and edges. Too little and the pastry will be dry; too much and the pastry will be greasy. You will master this after a few recipes. Some people prefer to use clarified butter which generally gives better results; clarified butter is melted butter which has had the milk solids skimmed off or filtered. See a general cookbook for detailed directions.

Shapes and sizes are suggested for recipes in this book; however, choose anything your creative heart desires. Generally, small squares, diamonds or triangles work well for appetizers, and you can enclose an entire roast within a phyllo crust.

PHYLLO PACKETS

This shape makes a nice main dish for lunch, brunch or casual entertaining entrées. Serve with soups or salads. Allow about ¼ to ⅓ cup filling for each packet.

Use 1 full sheet of phyllo per packet. Butter each sheet and fold in half lengthwise. Butter again. Place filling on a corner of the sheet. Fold over corner to the other side, as you would a flag. Place on a rimmed baking sheet and brush top with butter. (May be covered with plastic wrap at this point or frozen.) Bake at 375° for 15 to 20 minutes.

PHYLLO TRIANGLES

Very much like packets, but smaller. Cut stack of 5 sheets of phyllo lengthwise into 5 strips. Working with 1 strip at a time, brush lightly with melted butter. Place 1 rounded teaspoon of filling at the end of the strip. Fold one corner of the strip diagonally over the filling. Continue folding over at right angles until you reach the end of the strip. Bake at 375° for 10 to 15 minutes. Makes 5.

STRUDELS

12 sheets phyllo
$\frac{1}{2}$ cup butter, melted

Strudels are a wonderful shape for desserts, vegetables or main courses. They are bigger and contain more filling than appetizer phyllo "rolls." Unwrap phyllo sheets and cover with a slightly damp towel. To facilitate rolling, place a large clean dish towel on your work surface. Lay a phyllo sheet on the towel lengthwise and brush lightly with butter. Place a second sheet next to the first, overlapping edges by 3 inches. Repeat with remaining sheets. You will have a very large

square. Spread filling over the center of the buttered phyllo sheets, leaving a 2-inch border around the edge. Fold in edges. From the end closest to you, roll up strudel, jelly roll-style, using the towel to help you. With the towel for support, place strudel seam side down on a greased baking sheet with a rim. Brush top with butter.

Most strudels are baked at 375° for about 30 to 60 minutes, depending on filling. Check at 40 minutes to see if it is puffed and golden. Strudels are best served from the oven or warmed.

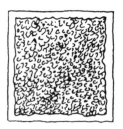
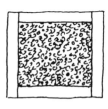
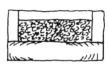

PHYLLO ROLLS

Cut a stack of 6 sheets crosswise into 4 strips. Working with 1 strip at a time, brush lightly with butter. Place 1 rounded teaspoon of filling in the center of bottom edge of the strip. Roll up ⅓ of the way and fold sides over roll. Continue rolling to the end. Bake at 375° for 10 to 15 minutes. Makes 24.

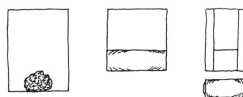

PHYLLO BUNDLES

Cut a stack of 5 sheets of phyllo lengthwise into 4 strips. Cut each strip crosswise into 5 squares. Place 2 squares on top of each other and brush lightly with melted butter. Layer 2 squares crosswise over the first 2 and brush with butter. Place 1 rounded teaspoon of filling in the center. Crimp phyllo around filling to make bundle. Bake at 375° for 10 to 15 minutes. Makes 10.

PHYLLO CUPS

8 sheets phyllo
½ cup butter, melted

To make this phyllo shape, you need miniature muffin tins with 12 cups, each about 1½ inches wide. Teflon-lined are the best. Fill these charming cups with savory appetizer fillings or sweet dessert mixtures. Using a piping bag to fill these does not work well. A small teaspoon seems to work best.

Brush a sheet of phyllo lightly with butter; repeat 5 times. Cut phyllo lengthwise into 4 strips. Cut each strip crosswise into 5 squares. Press each 2-inch square into a miniature muffin cup, flaring the sides out. Brush a phyllo sheet lightly with butter. Repeat 3 times, making 4 layers total. Using a sharp knife, make 5 lengthwise cuts and 3 crosswise cuts, evenly spaced. You will have 24 squares. Repeat to use 8 sheets of phyllo. Press each square into a muffin cup. Heat oven to 400° and bake for 8 to 12 minutes; watch carefully so they don't burn. Let cool and remove from pans. Store at room temperature and fill as desired. Makes 48.

PHYLLO SLICES

When you are making phyllo appetizers for a crowd, these are quicker and easier to do than individual appetizers. For each roll, lay out 1 full sheet of phyllo, butter it lightly and top with a second sheet. Repeat twice. Spread about 1 cup filling along the lengthwise edge. Roll up as you would a jelly roll. Tuck ends under roll. Place on a lightly buttered cookie sheet with a rim, seam side down. (May be covered and refrigerated at this point or frozen.) Brush rolls with melted butter and lightly score the top with a sharp knife into bite-sized slices. Bake at 375° for 20 minutes or until golden brown. Cut into slices and serve hot. Makes 15 to 18 slices per roll.

PHYLLO PIE CRUST, BOTTOM

8 sheets phyllo
½ cup butter, melted

This extraordinary crust can transform an ordinary dessert into something spectacular! Lightly grease a springform pan or metal quiche pan with a removable bottom. Brush a phyllo sheet lightly with butter and place it in the bottom of the pan. Fold edges over. You

don't have to be precise; it looks rather like a big crunchy hat when done! Continue adding the phyllo sheets, layering and brushing with butter as you go. Heat oven to 425° and bake for 15 to 20 minutes or until golden. Let cool and remove from pan. Store at room temperature for up to 2 days.

Use any filling that has already been prepared and spoon it into the prebaked crust just before serving. Sweet mixtures include mousses, puddings, ice cream or sweetened fresh fruits with whipped cream. Savory mixtures include creamed dishes, such as chicken in a cream sauce, vegetables in a cheese sauce or scrambled eggs.

PHYLLO PIE CRUST, DOUBLE

12 sheets phyllo
1/2 cup butter, melted

This shaping method results in a sweet or savory casserole-type dish, similar to a fruit crisp or a savory pie. Try it with your favorite fruit pie filling or quiche filling.

Heat oven to 375°. Brush a 9-x-13-inch baking pan lightly with butter. Prepare filling as desired and set aside. Layer 6 buttered

sheets of phyllo in the pan. Trim with scissors to 1 inch from edge of pan. Spread filling in pan and top with 6 more buttered sheets of phyllo. Cut edges to 1 inch from edge of pan and fold over to form a rim. Brush the top with butter and cut 3 vents in the top with a sharp knife; they should go through the top layers of phyllo into the filling. Bake for 50 to 60 minutes. Let pie rest for 10 minutes before cutting into squares or wedges to serve.

PHYLLO POUCHES OR KISSES

3 sheets phyllo
1/4 cup butter, melted

This way of shaping phyllo is quick and easy. You can use any type of filling you find in this book, as well as the recipes specifically designed for pouches. One package of phyllo will yield about 36 pouches.

Place a sheet of phyllo on your work surface and brush lightly with butter. Repeat twice to form a stack 3 sheets high. Cut the stack into four 6-inch squares. Place 1 rounded tablespoon of filling in the

center of each square. Gather up all sides to form a pouch. Pinch tightly in the center and down seams to seal. Arrange pouches on a buttered rimmed baking sheet and brush individually with butter. Bake at 400° for about 10 to 15 minutes or until golden.

NAPOLEON RECTANGLES

8 sheets phyllo
½ cup butter, melted
2 tbs. sugar, optional for *sweet* versions only

Heat oven to 350°. Place a sheet of phyllo on your work surface and brush with butter. Sprinkle with sugar for a sweet dessert. Repeat layering 3 times; you will have a stack 4 sheets high. With a sharp knife, make 2 cuts lengthwise and 3 cuts crosswise. You will have 12 rectangles. Place on a rimmed cookie sheet. Repeat with remaining phyllo. Bake rectangles for 12 to 15 minutes or until golden. May be stored at room temperature for 2 days in an airtight container or wrapped tightly in foil and frozen. Thaw unwrapped at room temperature. Makes 8 Napoleons, 3 rectangles per person, or 12 Napoleons, 2 rectangles per person.

CHICKEN CHUTNEY FILLING

*A food processor makes assembling this filling a snap.
Toast almonds in a 350° oven for 10 minutes.*

8 oz. cream cheese, softened
1/4 cup mayonnaise
1 1/2 cups diced cooked chicken
2 tbs. chutney
1 tsp. curry powder
2 green onions, sliced
1/4 tsp. white pepper
1/4 cup slivered almonds, toasted

With a food processor, combine cream cheese and mayonnaise until smooth. Add other ingredients and process until well mixed. Fill phyllo as desired.

Makes 60

CHINESE CRAB AND PORK FILLING

*Be sure to pick over crab to remove any bits of shell or cartilage.
Store the tuberous root, ginger, in the refrigerator in a glass jar
covered with sherry. It can also be frozen.*

1 lb. lean ground pork
1 clove garlic, minced
½ tsp. salt
¾ cup crabmeat
¼ cup minced water chestnuts

3 green onions, minced
2 tsp. grated ginger root
2 tbs. soy sauce
1 egg, beaten

In a large skillet over medium high heat, cook pork and garlic until
pork is no longer pink. Break up any large chunks of pork; sprinkle
with salt. Drain off fat and place mixture in a bowl. Add remaining
ingredients and mix well. Cool before filling phyllo.

Makes about 48

SAVORY MUSHROOM FILLING

If you don't care for blue cheese, just leave it out or use another type of cheese.

2 tbs. butter
½ cup finely chopped onion
¾ lb. mushrooms, finely chopped
1 tsp. salt
½ tsp. pepper
1 tbs. lemon juice
2 tbs. flour
2 oz. blue cheese, crumbled

Melt butter in a large skillet over medium high heat. Cook onion until soft. Add mushrooms and sprinkle with salt, pepper and lemon juice. When mushrooms are tender, sprinkle with flour and stir to thicken. Add blue cheese and continue cooking until cheese is melted. Remove from heat and cool before filling phyllo.

Makes about 60

SPICY LAMB FILLING

*A wonderful combination of sweet, hot, spicy and flaky,
all in one bite! Your friends will be asking for the recipe.*

½ cup raisins
1 cup finely chopped onion
2 cloves garlic, minced
2 tbs. olive oil
1 lb. ground lamb
1 tsp. salt
1 tsp. pepper

½ tsp. cinnamon
⅛ tsp. cayenne pepper
¼ cup catsup
¼ cup honey
¼ cup slivered almonds,
    toasted, optional

Cover raisins with hot water and set aside to plump. In a large
skillet over medium high heat, cook onion and garlic in olive oil until
softened. Add lamb and seasonings and cook until lamb is no longer
pink. Drain off liquid. Drain raisins well and add to pan with catsup,
honey and almonds. Simmer for 5 minutes to blend flavors. Cool
before filling phyllo.

Makes about 48

MOZZARELLA AND SPINACH FILLING

*For a change of pace, try adding some chopped salami
or pepperoni to this filling.*

1 pkg. (10 oz.) frozen chopped spinach, thawed
1/2 cup chopped onion
1 clove garlic, minced
1 tbs. vegetable oil
1/2 cup chopped sun-dried tomatoes
1/4 cup pine nuts, toasted
1 cup shredded mozzarella cheese
1/2 cup shredded Parmesan cheese

Place spinach in a dishtowel and wring tightly over the sink to remove excess moisture. In a large skillet over medium high heat, cook onion and garlic in oil until soft. Add spinach and cook for 1 minute. Remove from heat and stir in other ingredients (cheeses will melt). Cool to fill phyllo.

Makes about 48

CRAB AND CREAM CHEESE FILLING

These are good dipped in a Chinese plum sauce.

½ lb. crabmeat, free of shell or
    cartilage
8 oz. cream cheese, softened
3 green onions, thinly sliced

½ tsp. horseradish
½ tsp. lemon juice
½ tsp. salt
dash Tabasco Sauce

In a bowl or food processor, combine all ingredients until blended but still chunky. Chill.

CRAB AND BRIE FILLING

Brie's white rind covering is edible, although we don't use it here.

½ lb. Brie cheese, well chilled
½ lb. crabmeat
1 tbs. finely chopped green onion

1 tsp. lemon juice
¼ tsp. salt
⅛ tsp. cayenne pepper

Remove most of the rind from Brie and discard. Cut Brie into small dice. Combine with remaining ingredients.

Each recipe makes about 48

SMOKED SALMON FILLING

You can use smoked trout or other fish in this recipe as well.

1/4 lb. smoked salmon
8 oz. cream cheese, softened
1 tsp. dill weed

3 tbs. thinly sliced chives or
green onions

With a food processor or by hand, combine all ingredients until well mixed. Smoked salmon should be finely flaked. Chill.

CURRIED SHRIMP FILLING

Use tiny bay shrimp, and if you don't care for curry, leave it out.

8 oz. cream cheese, softened
1/2 lb. bay shrimp

3 tbs. green onions, minced
2 tsp. curry powder

With a food processor or by hand, combine all ingredients until well mixed. Chill.

Each recipe makes about 36

CHEESE AND SPINACH FILLING

A bit of nutmeg and the crunch of pine nuts enhance this spinach filling. Pine nuts actually come from pine cones. They should be stored in the freezer because of their high oil content. Toasting greatly improves the flavor — bake on a cookie sheet at 350° for about 10 minutes.

8 oz. cream cheese, softened
½ tsp. salt
½ tsp. pepper
½ tsp. nutmeg
1 egg, beaten

1 pkg. (10 oz.) frozen chopped spinach, thawed
2 tbs. pine nuts, toasted, optional

With a food processor or an electric mixer, combine cream cheese with seasonings and egg until light and fluffy. Place spinach in a dishtowel and wring out moisture over the sink. Stir spinach and pine nuts into cream cheese.

Makes about 48

PEPPERED FETA FILLING

Use part skim milk ricotta for this filling.

8 oz. feta cheese
1 cup ricotta cheese
1/4 cup chopped fresh parsley

3/4 tsp. coarsely ground pepper
2 eggs, beaten

With a food processor or mixer, combine ingredients. Fill phyllo as desired.

Makes 75

ONION CHEESE FILLING

Perfect for appetizer strudels. You can add 3/4 tsp. caraway seeds.

3 tbs. butter
3 large onions, chopped

6 oz. cream cheese, softened
2 cups shredded Swiss cheese

In a large skillet over medium high heat, melt butter and cook onions until golden brown, about 20 minutes. Remove from heat and let cool to lukewarm. Combine with cheeses. Fill phyllo as desired.

Makes 60

ARTICHOKE FILLING

This recipe will fill about 100 appetizers that can be made ahead and frozen. Bake directly from the freezer without thawing. The breadcrumbs between the layers make them extra crispy.

2 tbs. butter
$\frac{1}{2}$ cup flour
1 cup milk
1 tsp. lemon juice
$\frac{1}{2}$ tsp. salt
$\frac{1}{4}$ tsp. white pepper
$\frac{1}{4}$ tsp. nutmeg

1 cup grated Parmesan cheese
1 cup shredded mozzarella
    cheese
2 pkg. (9 oz. each) frozen
    artichoke hearts, cooked,
    drained and chopped
3 tbs. Italian breadcrumbs

Melt butter in a saucepan over medium high heat, whisk in flour and add milk, lemon juice and seasonings. Cook until thickened and bubbly. Add sauce and cheeses to chopped artichokes and combine well. Refrigerate until cold. Fill phyllo as desired; sprinkle breadcrumbs on phyllo sheets after brushing with butter. Preheat oven to 400°. Bake for 15 to 20 minutes, or until golden.

Makes 100

BLUE CHEESE AND WALNUT FILLING

Adding an egg or breadcrumbs to a phyllo filling helps it firm up as it is baked. To toast walnuts and enhance the flavor, place nuts in a sieve and rinse with water. Shake thoroughly and place nuts on a cookie sheet. Bake at 350° for 10 minutes or until toasted.

8 oz. cream cheese, softened
1 egg
1/4 lb. crumbled blue cheese
1/2 cup coarsely chopped toasted walnuts
1 can (4 oz.) chopped ripe olives, well drained
1/4 tsp. nutmeg
1/4 tsp. pepper

With a food processor or by hand in a small bowl, combine cream cheese and egg until evenly blended. Stir in blue cheese, walnuts and olives. Season to taste with nutmeg and pepper. Fill phyllo as desired.

Makes 30

CARAMELIZED ONION FILLING

Use this delicious filling in phyllo rolls, pouches, triangles or cups.

1/4 cup butter
2 cups chopped onion
1 tsp. sugar
8 oz. cream cheese, softened
1 egg, beaten
Tabasco Sauce to taste
3 tbs. grated Parmesan cheese
1 cup shredded Monterey Jack cheese

Melt butter in a large skillet over medium high heat. Add onion and cook until soft, sprinkle with sugar and continue cooking until onions are golden brown and caramelized. Remove from skillet to a bowl and let cool. Combine cream cheese, egg, Tabasco and Parmesan until smooth. Stir in onions and shredded cheese. Chill. Fill phyllo as desired.

Makes about 48

TYROPITTA FILLING

This Middle Eastern filling is traditionally shaped in a triangle, but you can use any method you wish.

4 oz. feta cheese
4 oz. cream cheese, softened
1 egg, beaten
2 tbs. finely chopped fresh parsley
$\frac{1}{2}$ tsp. dill
$\frac{1}{4}$ tsp. white pepper

With a food processor or an electric mixer, combine cheeses and egg until smooth. Add parsley, dill and pepper. Chill. Fill phyllo as desired.

Makes about 48

BAKED SPRING ROLLS

Oriental dark sesame oil is a flavoring oil and should be kept in the refrigerator. Bean sprouts should be kept in a plastic container covered with cold water in the refrigerator. Change the water every day or two. These excellent appetizers freeze well.

1 tbs. finely chopped ginger root
2 cloves garlic, minced
2 tbs. sesame oil
1 tbs. vegetable oil
2 cups fresh bean sprouts
¾ lb. raw shrimp, peeled and deveined
1 can (8 oz.) water chestnuts, chopped

¼ lb. lean ham, minced
½ cup sliced green onions
½ cup shredded carrot
2 tsp. cornstarch
2 tbs. water
1 tbs. soy sauce
15 sheets phyllo
1 cup butter, melted
1 tbs. sesame seeds

In a large skillet over medium high heat, stir-fry ginger and garlic in oils for 30 seconds. Add bean sprouts, shrimp, water chestnuts, ham, green onions and carrot; cook, stirring constantly, for 2 minutes. Combine cornstarch and water and add to vegetable mixture with soy sauce. Stir until thickened. Remove from heat and cool.

To form spring rolls, cut phyllo sheets in half crosswise. Fold in the short end of each piece to form a square. Cover remaining phyllo with plastic wrap and a damp towel. Brush square lightly with melted butter and turn so the corner faces you. Spoon 1 tablespoon of the filling on the corner and fold over to enclose. Fold over again, and fold sides to the center to form an envelope shape. Continue rolling phyllo to form a roll. Place seam side down on a baking sheet. Brush with butter and sprinkle with sesame seeds. Repeat with remaining phyllo and filling. (May be refrigerated or frozen at this point.)

To bake, preheat oven to 375°. Bake for 10 to 15 minutes or until browned. Serve warm.

Makes 30

GARLIC CHICKEN ROLLS

Experiment with different dips; ranch dressing is good.

2 whole chicken breasts,
  skinned and boned
3 tbs. lemon juice
3 tbs. olive oil
3 cloves garlic, minced

1 tsp. crumbled oregano
½ tsp. dill
½ tsp. salt
½ cup butter, melted
½ pkg. phyllo, thawed

Cut chicken into ¾-inch cubes. In a glass bowl, combine lemon juice, oil, garlic and seasonings; stir well. Add chicken cubes and refrigerate overnight.

Preheat oven to 400°. Cut phyllo in half lengthwise. Cover remaining sheets with plastic wrap and a damp towel while working with each sheet. Brush sheet with butter and fold in half crosswise. Place 2 pieces of chicken at the short end of phyllo. Roll up to midpoint. Fold sides over to enclose filling and continue rolling to the end. Place seam side down on a rimmed cookie sheet. Brush with butter. Repeat with remaining chicken and phyllo. Bake for 20 minutes.

Makes 8 servings

BAKED BRIE IN PHYLLO

Use only a whole uncut wheel of Brie with the rind. Serve with mild crackers and fresh fruit, such as apples, pears and grapes.

12 sheets phyllo
½ cup butter, melted

1 wheel of Brie cheese, 1½ lb.
½ cup slivered almonds, toasted

Lightly brush 1 phyllo sheet with butter, lay a second sheet on top and place wheel of Brie in the center. Gently press almonds into cheese. Fold phyllo around cheese. Brush another phyllo sheet lightly with butter and top with a second sheet. Turn cheese upside down and place in center of sheet, folding phyllo around cheese to completely enclose. Keep repeating with remaining 8 sheets of phyllo. Place cheese on a rimmed baking sheet and refrigerate for 10 minutes. Heat oven to 375°. Brush top of phyllo lightly with butter and bake for 15 to 20 minutes or until puffed and golden. Let stand for 15 minutes before serving.

Makes 12 servings

BAKED BRIE WITH WILD MUSHROOMS

This is a spectacular appetizer for a special party. This recipe makes enough for 20 to 25 guests. Accompany with sliced French bread. You could also use the mushroom mixture to make phyllo pouches or kisses.

6 oz. fresh chantrelle mushrooms, rinsed and dried
6 oz. fresh shiitake mushrooms, rinsed and dried
3 tbs. butter
3 green onions, thinly sliced
6 oz. fresh button mushrooms, sliced lengthwise
1/4 cup tawny port wine
1/2 tsp. thyme
1/2 tsp. marjoram
1 tsp. salt
1/2 tsp. pepper
12 sheets phyllo
1/2 cup butter, melted
1 wheel of Brie cheese, 5 lb.

Mince chantrelle and shiitake mushrooms. Heat 3 tbs. butter in a heavy skillet over medium high heat. Cook green onions until tender. Add dried and fresh mushrooms and cook until tender. Add wine and cook until it evaporates. Season with herbs, salt and pepper. Remove mixture from skillet and cool.

Place a sheet of phyllo vertically on your work surface and brush lightly with butter; place another sheet side by side, overlapping by 2 inches to form a large square. Repeat twice using 6 sheets total. Place Brie in center of phyllo square and top with cooled mushroom mixture. Bring edges up and fold over top of cheese and mushrooms. Repeat procedure, making another square of phyllo using 6 sheets total. Lift and place on top of phyllo-wrapped cheese. Transfer to a rimmed baking sheet and tuck ends of phyllo under cheese to enclose completely.

Preheat oven to 350°. Bake Brie for 20 to 30 minutes or until golden. Let stand for 30 minutes before serving. Transfer to a platter and cut into wedges to serve.

Makes 20-25 servings

SMOKED SALMON NAPOLEON

Elegant! Use only the mildest, sweetest onion you can find.

8 oz. cold smoked salmon
1 large sweet onion
16 Napoleon rectangles, page 12

1½ cups sour cream
black sesame seeds for garnish

Cut salmon into slivers. Cut onion vertically into slivers. To assemble, place 1 phyllo rectangle on 8 salad plates. Scatter onion slivers on top and over sides of phyllo. Top with a spoonful of sour cream and ⅛ of the smoked salmon. Top with another rectangle of phyllo and a small dollop of sour cream. Sprinkle with black sesame seeds. Serve immediately.

Makes 8 servings

NAPOLEON VARIATIONS

- Layer Napoleon rectangles with fresh blanched asparagus and a nippy cheese sauce.

- Layer Napoleon rectangles with cooked artichoke hearts and creamed seafood.

PHYLLO PIZZA

You can use any of your favorite pizza toppings. This makes a great appetizer when cut into small squares.

7 sheets phyllo
1/3 cup butter, melted
1/4 cup grated Parmesan cheese
1 cup shredded mozzarella cheese
1 red onion, thinly sliced

3 tomatoes, thinly sliced
1/2 tsp. crumbled oregano
1/2 tsp. thyme
1/4 cup sliced ripe olives
1/2 cup thinly sliced green bell pepper

Heat oven to 375°. Place 1 sheet of phyllo on a rimmed baking sheet. Cover remaining phyllo with plastic wrap and a damp towel. Brush phyllo lightly with butter and sprinkle with some Parmesan. Repeat with remaining phyllo, butter and Parmesan. Sprinkle top sheet with mozzarella. Arrange onion slices over cheese and top with tomatoes. Sprinkle with oregano and thyme. Scatter olives and green pepper over the top. Bake for 20 to 30 minutes or until browned.

Makes 8 servings

CHICKEN BREASTS WITH SPINACH FILLING

A very impressive entrée for a dinner party, these can be made ahead and frozen for up to 2 weeks before serving. This is one phyllo recipe you must defrost first. Walnuts add a nice crunch and green peppercorns add a nice edge — you'll find them at the grocery store near the condiments. They are unripe black peppercorns, packed in brine and sold in small bottles.

SPINACH FILLING

1 pkg. (10 oz.) frozen chopped spinach, thawed
1 cup shredded Swiss cheese
4 oz. cream cheese
½ cup finely chopped onion

½ cup chopped toasted walnuts
2 tbs. green peppercorns, rinsed and drained
½ tsp. salt
½ tsp. pepper

4 large chicken breasts, skinned and boned

½ pkg. phyllo, thawed
½ cup butter, melted

Squeeze excess moisture out of thawed spinach by placing it in a dishtowel and wringing it over the sink. In a small bowl, combine spinach filling ingredients until evenly mixed. Cut chicken breasts in half, place about ⅓ cup of filling in the center of each, and roll up to enclose filling.

Place 1 sheet of phyllo on your work surface. Keep others covered with plastic wrap and a damp towel. Brush phyllo with melted butter and fold in half widthwise. Turn phyllo with narrow end facing you, place chicken on the bottom edge at the center. Roll chicken over once and fold in the sides. Continue rolling phyllo to end, placing bundle seam side down on a rimmed baking sheet. Brush top with butter. Repeat with remaining chicken and phyllo. (May be refrigerated overnight at this point, or frozen for up to 2 weeks.)

Before baking, thaw chicken to room temperature. Preheat oven to 400°. Bake for 25 to 30 minutes or until golden.

Makes 8 servings

FILET OF BEEF IN PHYLLO

Sure to impress any guest, this elegant entrée has a sauce that makes a perfect counterpoint. Serve with a simple green salad and glazed carrots.

1 whole beef filet mignon,
   about 3 lb.
1 tsp. salt
2 tbs. butter

1 tbs. vegetable oil
12 sheets phyllo
½ cup butter, melted
Sauce, follows

Heat oven to 400°. Rub meat with salt. Heat butter and oil in a heavy skillet and sear meat over medium high heat until browned on all sides. Remove meat from pan and set aside. Reserve pan with juices. Brush each sheet of phyllo with butter, stacking sheets. Place beef on phyllo, fold ends over and roll to enclose meat completely. Place on a rimmed baking sheet and bake for 30 minutes, or until browned and flaky; meat will test at 130° with a meat thermometer. Remove to a platter and let stand for 10 minutes before slicing. Serve with sauce.

SAUCE

1 clove garlic, minced
2 large shallots, minced
½ cup chicken stock
½ cup dry vermouth
1 tbs. lemon juice
2 tsp. crumbled dried tarragon
½ cup heavy cream
salt and pepper

In pan with reserved juices, cook garlic and shallots until softened. Add chicken stock, vermouth, lemon juice and tarragon. Bring to a boil and scrape up any browned bits on the bottom. Add cream and continue to boil until sauce is thickened, about 2 minutes. Add salt and pepper to taste.

Makes 6 servings

LAMB PHYLLO WITH MUSHROOMS

This is an elegant presentation for a special cut of meat.
It will impress the most discriminating guest.

3½ lb. rack of lamb, boned, trimmed of fat
2 tsp. vegetable oil
1 tsp. salt
½ tsp. pepper
4 tbs. butter
½ lb. fresh mushrooms, finely chopped
3 shallots, finely chopped
4 sheets phyllo
1 egg, lightly beaten

In a large skillet over medium high heat, cook lamb in oil until browned on all sides, about 4 minutes. Sprinkle with salt and pepper. Remove from skillet and refrigerate until cold. Add 1 tbs. of the butter to pan and cook mushrooms and shallots until softened. Cool.

Preheat oven to 400°. Melt remaining 3 tbs. butter. Lay 1 sheet of phyllo on your work surface with short edge towards you. Brush lightly with butter and repeat with remaining phyllo. Spoon $\frac{1}{2}$ of the cooled mushroom mixture on bottom edge of phyllo in center, leaving a 2-inch border on sides. Place lamb on top of mushrooms, and top with remaining mushroom mixture. Fold in edges from long sides; roll up lamb in phyllo to 4 inches from the top. Brush phyllo with beaten egg and continue rolling.

Place on a rimmed baking sheet and brush top with remaining egg. Bake for 20 minutes; lamb will be medium rare. Let meat rest for 10 minutes. Slice into 4 slices.

Makes 4 servings

CHICKEN IN PHYLLO WITH MUSTARD AND GREEN PEPPERCORNS

Green peppercorns are unripe black peppercorns.
They are sold in the condiment section of your
grocery store, packed in brine in small jars.

1/4 cup butter
3 whole chicken breasts, skinned, boned and cut into pieces
1 tsp. salt
1/2 tsp. white pepper
1/2 cup Dijon mustard
2 cups heavy cream
1 tbs. green peppercorns, drained
6 phyllo sheets
1/2 cup butter, melted
1/4 cup fine dry breadcrumbs
1 egg yolk mixed with 1 tbs. water

Melt butter in a large skillet and cook chicken pieces until no longer pink; sprinkle with salt and pepper. Do not overcook. Remove from skillet and set aside. Add mustard to pan and scrape up any brown bits. Add cream and bring to a boil. Reduce heat and simmer until reduced to 1 cup. Add green peppercorns. Pour sauce over chicken pieces and let cool.

Preheat oven to 425°. Lay 1 sheet of phyllo on your work surface, brush lightly with melted butter and sprinkle with crumbs. Repeat 5 times. Place chicken at the bottom edge of the long side of phyllo. Fold over edges and roll up like a jelly roll. Place on a rimmed baking sheet, seam side down. Brush with egg and water mixture. Bake for 15 minutes or until golden. Cut into 6 slices to serve.

Makes 6 servings

SAUSAGE AND MUSHROOM STRUDEL

A savory strudel is a very special entrée for brunch. Serve it with something simple, such as scrambled eggs. This recipe makes 3 strudels, each serving 2 to 3 persons.

16 oz. lean pork sausage
½ lb. mushrooms, coarsely chopped
4 green onions, thinly sliced
8 oz. cream cheese, cubed
18 sheets phyllo
½ cup butter, melted
½ cup fine dry breadcrumbs

Preheat oven to 400°. Cook sausage in a large skillet until it loses most of its pinkness. Drain off fat, add mushrooms and green onions to skillet and continue cooking until sausage is done. Drain off any excess liquid. Add cream cheese to skillet and stir until blended. Remove from heat and set filling aside.

Place a sheet of phyllo on your work surface. Cover remaining sheets with plastic wrap and a damp dish towel. Brush sheet with butter and sprinkle with breadcrumbs. Repeat 5 times until you have 6 sheets. Place 1/3 of the filling mixture on the short side of the phyllo and fold ends over to make an envelope. Roll up completely, brush top with butter and score lightly on the diagonal with a sharp knife, about 3 times. Place on an ungreased cookie sheet. Repeat procedure for the second and third strudels.

Bake for 20 minutes or until golden brown. Slice crosswise to serve.

Makes 6-9 servings

EGGPLANT AND SAUSAGE PIE

If you'd like, ground beef or lamb are also good in this dish.

1 eggplant, about 1 lb.
1 tbs. salt
2 tbs. olive oil
1 lb. sausage, casings removed
2 tbs. tomato paste
1 tsp. marjoram
1 tsp. thyme
2 cups ricotta cheese
2 eggs, beaten
3 cloves garlic, minced
8 oz. mozzarella, shredded
1/3 cup grated Parmesan cheese
1 tsp. salt
1/2 tsp. pepper
phyllo and melted butter for phyllo pie crust, double, page 10

Cut eggplant, with skin on, into ¾-inch dice. Place in a colander, sprinkle with 1 tbs. salt and let stand for 1 hour. Rinse with cold water and pat dry.

Heat olive oil in a large skillet over medium high heat, add sausage and cook until no longer pink. With a slotted spoon, remove sausage from skillet and set aside. Add eggplant to pan and cook until soft. Add tomato paste and sausage; season with marjoram and thyme. Remove from pan and cool. With a food processor or an electric mixer, combine ricotta, eggs, garlic, cheeses, salt and pepper until well mixed.

Preheat oven to 375°. Prepare phyllo as directed for phyllo pie. Spoon sausage and eggplant mixture into pan. Top with cheese mixture, spreading evenly. Top with remaining phyllo as directed. Bake for 50 to 60 minutes. Let stand for 10 minutes before cutting.

Makes 8-10 servings

CHICKEN AND VEGETABLE PIE

You can use a variety of vegetables in this pie — for example,
asparagus, broccoli, spinach or zucchini.

2 tbs. butter
½ cup chopped onion
1 clove garlic, minced
2 cups sliced fresh mushrooms
½ cup sherry
⅛ tsp. nutmeg
½ tsp. salt
¼ tsp. pepper
3 cups diced cooked chicken
2 cups chopped cooked broccoli, zucchini or spinach, well drained,
or shredded uncooked zucchini, unpeeled
½ cup sour cream
2 eggs, beaten
¼ tsp. thyme
¼ tsp. marjoram

phyllo and melted butter for phyllo pie crust,
double, page 10

Melt butter in a heavy skillet over medium high heat. Cook onion
and garlic until onion is soft. Add mushrooms and cook until tender.
Add sherry and seasonings and cook until sherry evaporates. Remove
from heat and place mixture in a large bowl. Cool.

Add chicken, broccoli, sour cream, eggs, thyme and marjoram.
Make pie according to directions.

Makes 8-10 servings

KING SALMON IN PHYLLO

Salmon is always special, and wrapping it in phyllo
makes it a very special dish indeed.

6 sheets phyllo
¼ cup butter, melted
4 king salmon fillets, about 6 oz. each
¼ cup prepared pesto
½ cup chopped sun-dried tomatoes

Preheat oven to 350°. Brush each sheet of phyllo lightly with butter, and stack them 3 sheets high. Cut in half horizontally, making 4 stacks. Place salmon fillet in the center of the bottom edge of each stack. Spread each with ¼ of the pesto and top with sun-dried tomatoes. Fold sides of phyllo over salmon and roll each fillet over to completely enclose fillet. Place on a rimmed cookie sheet and brush top with butter. Bake for 15 minutes or until pastry is golden brown.

Makes 4 servings

SPANAKOPITA

Use this Greek favorite as a side dish, a vegetarian entrée or an appetizer. It can be refrigerated or frozen before baking.

1 cup chopped onion
2 tbs. butter
8 oz. feta cheese
4 oz. cream cheese
2 eggs
2 tbs. chopped fresh parsley
1 tsp. nutmeg

1 cup shredded Monterey Jack cheese
1 pkg. (10 oz.) frozen chopped spinach, thawed, squeezed dry
½ pkg. phyllo, thawed
½ cup butter, melted

In a large skillet over medium high heat, cook onion in butter until soft. With a food processor or electric mixer, combine cheeses, eggs, parsley and nutmeg. Add Jack cheese and spinach and combine. Heat oven to 350°. Butter a 9-x-13-inch baking dish and place a sheet of phyllo on the bottom. Brush lightly with butter and layer with 12 buttered sheets of phyllo. Spread with filling and cover with 12 additional buttered sheets. Score the top into 8 squares with a sharp knife. Bake at 350° for 45 minutes or until brown and top is crispy.

Makes 8 servings

BASIC ENTRÉE STRUDEL

This recipe is a basic place to start; you can add vegetables, seafood, chicken or meats that appeal to you.

2 tbs. butter
1 cup chopped onion
8 oz. cream cheese
2 cups shredded Monterey Jack
   cheese
3 tbs. grated Parmesan cheese

3 eggs, beaten
1 tsp. salt
½ tsp. pepper
melted butter and phyllo for
   strudel, page 5

Melt butter in a large skillet over medium high heat and cook onion until soft. Remove to a bowl. With a food processor or electric mixer, combine cheeses and eggs until smooth. Add onion, salt and pepper. Add 1 or a combination from the following list, and follow directions for making and baking strudel on page 5.

- 1 pkg. (10 oz.) frozen chopped spinach, thawed and squeezed dry, with 1 tsp. nutmeg

- 1 pkg. (10 oz.) frozen chopped broccoli, cooked and well drained
- 4 cups shredded zucchini, unpeeled (place in a sieve, sprinkle with salt and let stand for 30 minutes; squeeze very dry)
- ¾ lb. chopped mushrooms, cooked until tender in 2 tbs. butter
- ½ head cabbage, chopped and sautéed in 2 tbs. butter
- ½ cup shredded carrot
- ½ cup chopped seeded tomato
- 1 cup diced cooked chicken or turkey
- 1 cup baby shrimp
- ½ cup crumbled crisp bacon
- 1 cup chopped ham

ARTICHOKE PIE

Try substituting cheddar cheese for the Swiss and adding 1 cup of chopped ham or proscuitto to this recipe. You can cut this into smaller squares and use it as an appetizer.

2 cups chopped marinated artichokes, well drained
1 lb. ricotta cheese
$\frac{1}{2}$ cup sour cream
4 eggs, beaten
$\frac{3}{4}$ cup thinly sliced green onions
$\frac{3}{4}$ cup grated Parmesan cheese
1 cup shredded Swiss cheese
2 tsp. dried basil
$\frac{1}{2}$ tsp. salt
$\frac{1}{2}$ tsp. pepper
phyllo and melted butter for phyllo pie crust, double, page 10

In a large mixing bowl, combine all ingredients. Follow directions for phyllo pie.

Makes 8-10 entrée servings, 16 appetizer servings

STRAWBERRIES AND CUSTARD NAPOLEON

*A visual delight! Try other fresh berries or fruit in season, such as
raspberries or peaches. Packaged pudding mix saves time.*

1 pkg. (6⅛ oz.) instant vanilla
  pudding mix
2 pints fresh strawberries
sugar
1 cup whipping cream

¼ cup powdered sugar
1 tsp. vanilla extract
24 Napoleon rectangles, sweet
  version, page 12

Make pudding according to package directions and chill. Prepare
strawberries by washing, hulling and slicing. Place in a bowl and add
sugar to taste. Chill. Whip cream until soft; add powdered sugar and
vanilla.

To assemble desserts, place 1 rectangle on a pretty dessert plate,
spread with 1 tbs. of the pudding, and top with another rectangle.
Spoon ⅛ of the berries over top, add another rectangle and top with
whipped cream. Serve immediately.

Makes 8 servings

BOREKIAS

This is a classic Middle Eastern pastry. Orange flower water is available in drugstores, gourmet cooking stores and the liquor store. Serve this unusual cheesecake-like dessert for a dinner party when lamb is the main course.

1 pkg. (1 lb.) phyllo, thawed
1 cup butter, melted

FILLING

16 oz. cream cheese, softened
¼ cup honey
2 tbs. sugar
1 tsp. cinnamon

Heat oven to 325°. Brush a 9-inch square baking pan with butter. Place 1 sheet of phyllo in the bottom of the pan and brush lightly with butter. Fold in edges to fit pan. Repeat 9 times. Combine ingredients for filling with a food processor or electric mixer. Spread filling over

sheets in pan. Repeat layering phyllo sheets and brushing with butter 10 more times. With a sharp knife, cut top phyllo sheets lengthwise into 2-inch strips. Cut diagonally across strips to make diamond shapes. Bake for 30 minutes; increase temperature to 450° and bake for 15 minutes longer, until puffed and golden. Make syrup. Pour hot syrup immediately over baked borekias after removing from oven. Let cool completely. Cut along scored lines. Serve the same day at room temperature.

SYRUP

1 cup honey
1 cup water
1 tbs. orange flower water

Combine honey and water in a saucepan . Bring to a boil, stirring until honey is dissolved. Simmer mixture until it thickens and coats the back of a spoon. Add orange flower water.

Makes 16

TRADITIONAL BAKLAVA

*The method is actually quite easy to make – almost like lasagna.
Assemble the tools first: a 9-x-13-inch metal pan, plastic wrap, a
dish towel, a sharp paring knife, scissors and paper cupcake liners.*

PHYLLO LAYERS

1 pkg. (1 lb.) phyllo, thawed   1 lb. butter, melted

NUT FILLING

4 cups finely chopped walnuts   1 tbs. grated lemon peel
¾ cup sugar   3 tbs. cinnamon

SYRUP

1½ cups honey   1 lemon, seeded and cut into
1½ cups sugar   quarters
1 cup water

With a food processor, combine filling ingredients until nuts are
finely chopped. Set aside. On your work surface, place a sheet of

phyllo. Cover remaining phyllo with plastic wrap and a damp kitchen towel. Brush sheet lightly with butter. Brush pan with butter. Top buttered sheet with another phyllo sheet and place both in pan; smooth into corners to avoid air pockets. Repeat 5 times, brushing each second sheet with butter (12 sheets in all). Spread ½ of the nut mixture over phyllo layers. Top with 4 phyllo sheets, buttering every second sheet. Spread with remaining nut mixture.

Repeat double layers of phyllo sheets 6 times (total 12 sheets.) With scissors, trim excess phyllo hanging over edges of pan. Brush top with butter. Refrigerate for 15 minutes to solidify butter. With a sharp knife, score top layers of phyllo into diamond shapes, going into nut mixture. Heat oven to 350° and bake for 45 to 55 minutes, or until golden. Do not underbake.

Combine syrup ingredients in a saucepan over medium high heat. Bring to a boil, reduce heat and simmer for 20 minutes. Skim off any bubbles or scum; remove lemon pieces and discard. Pour hot syrup over cooled baklava. When completely cool, finish cutting, place each piece in a paper cupcake liner, and serve at room temperature.

Makes about 36

MIXED NUT BAKLAVA

This is a delicious variation of traditional baklava. To toast coconut, spread coconut on a cookie sheet and bake in a 350° oven for 5 to 10 minutes, stirring twice to break up clumps and redistribute coconut so that it toasts evenly.
Watch carefully so it does not burn.

1 pkg. (1 lb.) phyllo, thawed
1¼ cups butter, melted
1¼ cups coconut, toasted
¼ cup chopped macadamia nuts
½ cup chopped pecans

½ cup brown sugar
1 tsp. allspice
1 cup sugar
½ cup water
¼ cup honey

Heat oven to 350° and butter a 9-x-13-inch baking pan. Cut phyllo sheets in half crosswise. Cover phyllo with plastic wrap and a damp towel. Layer 10 sheets of phyllo in pan, brushing each sheet lightly with butter. Combine coconut, nuts, brown sugar and allspice. Sprinkle ⅓ of the mixture over phyllo. Repeat layering 10 sheets of phyllo

and 1/3 of the coconut-nut mixture twice more, and end with buttered phyllo.

Score top layers of phyllo with a sharp knife into diamond shapes. First make cuts lengthwise about every 2 inches, and cut crosswise on the diagonal to form diamond shapes. Be sure to cut all the way through layers of phyllo down to nut mixture. Bake for 45 minutes or until top is browned. Let cool completely.

Make sugar syrup: Combine sugar, water and honey in a saucepan over medium high heat. Bring to a boil, reduce heat and simmer for 5 minutes. Remove from heat and drizzle over baklava. Cover and let stand at room temperature for 24 hours before serving.

Makes about 36

PINEAPPLE BAKLAVA

*Rich and delicious, this is similar to a recipe that won
first prize in a cooking contest years ago.*

1 can (1 lb. 14 oz.) crushed pineapple in syrup
8 oz. cream cheese, softened
1 cup ricotta cheese
½ cup sugar
2 egg yolks
1 tsp. grated lemon peel
1 tsp. vanilla extract
12 sheets phyllo
½ cup butter, melted
½ cup sugar
1 tsp. lemon juice

Drain pineapple and reserve syrup. With a food processor or an electric mixer, combine cream cheese, ricotta, sugar, egg yolks, lemon peel and vanilla until light. Stir in pineapple and set aside.

Lightly butter a 9-x-13-inch baking pan. Layer 1 sheet of phyllo on the bottom, and fold edges over. Repeat 5 times, brushing each layer lightly with butter. Heat oven to 350°. Bake first layer of phyllo for 15 minutes. Remove from oven, but leave oven on.

Spread with pineapple cream cheese mixture. Top with a sheet of phyllo, brush lightly with butter and repeat 5 times. Score top into squares with the tip of a sharp knife; do not cut all the way through to filling. Make 4 cuts lengthwise and 5 cuts crosswise. Return to oven and bake for 40 minutes, or until golden.

Make syrup: Combine ½ cup reserved pineapple syrup, sugar and lemon juice in a small saucepan over high heat. Bring to a boil and boil for 10 minutes or until thickened. Spoon hot syrup over top of hot baklava. Cut through markings into squares. Serve warm.

Makes 30

APPLE BAKLAVA

Serve this elegant dessert on a beautiful cake pedestal.
Use a very sharp knife to cut the layers.

APPLE FILLING

2 tbs. butter
2 lb. Golden Delicious apples,
   peeled and cored, cut into
   1/4-inch slices to measure
   about 6 cups

3 tbs. brown sugar
1 tsp. cinnamon
1/4 tsp. allspice
1/2 cup apple juice

PHYLLO LAYERS

1/2 cup ground walnuts or
   almonds
1/4 cup sugar
16 sheets phyllo

1/4 cup butter, melted
1 cup caramel ice cream
   topping
2 tbs. powdered sugar

To make apple filling: Melt butter in a large skillet over medium high heat, add apples, sugar and spices and cook, stirring, until

apples begin to soften. Add juice and simmer for 10 minutes or until apples are tender and mixture is thickened.

To make phyllo layers: With a food processor, combine nuts and sugar until finely ground. Prepare phyllo sheets by stacking all phyllo sheets on top of each other. With an 8-inch plate as a guide, in each corner of phyllo, cut around plate through all layers with a sharp knife to make 4 stacks of circles. You will have 32 circles. Cover phyllo circles with a piece of plastic wrap and a damp dish towel.

Preheat oven to 375°. Grease 2 cookie sheets. Place 1 phyllo circle in the corner of the cookie sheet and brush lightly with butter. Sprinkle with 2 tsp. of the nut mixture and repeat to make stack 8 layers thick. Repeat with remaining dough, making 4 phyllo stacks in all. Bake for 10 minutes or until golden. Remove to a wire rack to cool.

To assemble: Stack 1 phyllo layer on a plate, top with 1 cup of the apple filling, drizzle with 2 tbs. caramel sauce, and repeat, ending with a phyllo layer. Sprinkle top with powdered sugar. Serve at room temperature within 1 hour of assembly.

Makes 6-8 servings

ROLLED BAKLAVA

This method of preparation makes tiny 1-bite delights. If you can find them, individual paper candy cups make a nice way to display these treats. Baklava is always served at room temperature and keeps well in the refrigerator for about 10 days.

3 cups almonds, blanched
3 cups walnuts
1½ cups pecans
⅓ cup sugar
2 tbs. cinnamon

¾ tsp. nutmeg
¼ tsp. ground cloves
2 cups butter, melted
1 pkg. (1 lb.) phyllo, thawed

SYRUP

4½ cups water
3¾ cups sugar
2 small cinnamon sticks

1½ tsp. lemon juice
grated peel of 1 lemon
1 tbs. honey

Heat oven to 350°. Grind nuts finely with a food processor. Add sugar and spices. Place mixture in a bowl. Place phyllo on a work surface and cover with plastic wrap and a damp towel. Using 1 sheet of phyllo at a time, brush lightly with butter and sprinkle with 1/3 cup of the nut mixture, spreading evenly over surface of phyllo. Roll up tightly lengthwise into a cylinder shape. Brush seam lightly with butter to seal. Cut into 1-inch pieces. Butter a rimmed cookie sheet or jelly roll pan with sides. Place pieces cut end up on sheet, about 1/2-inch apart. Brush tops lightly with butter. Bake for 20 minutes or until golden. Cool at room temperature in pans.

To make syrup: Combine ingredients in a saucepan over medium high heat and bring to a boil. Turn heat to low and simmer for 10 minutes.

Spoon hot syrup over rolls when cool. Turn rolls over in syrup to absorb as much syrup as possible.

Makes about 200

PEAR AND RAISIN PIE WITH PHYLLO CRUST

*You can make a lighter version of this pie by using nonstick
cooking spray between the sheets of phyllo instead of butter.*

5 large ripe pears, about 2¾ lb.
1 cup raisins, optional
¼ cup apple juice
¼ cup sugar
¼ cup brown sugar
2 tbs. flour
2 tbs. lemon juice
¾ tsp. cinnamon
½ tsp. ground ginger
½ tsp. nutmeg
4 sheets phyllo
¼ cup butter, melted, or nonstick cooking spray
1 tsp. sugar

Preheat oven to 400°. Peel and core pears and cut into ½-inch-thick slices. Place pears, raisins, juice, sugars, flour, lemon juice and spices in a heavy large saucepan. Bring to a boil, reduce heat and simmer until pears are tender. Pour mixture into a 9-inch pie pan. Let cool.

Place 1 sheet of phyllo over pears and brush with butter, or spray. Place another layer crosswise over the first. Brush with butter and layer 2 more times. Brush top with butter and sprinkle with sugar. Place pie pan on a rimmed cookie sheet. Bake for 12 minutes or until golden. Cool on a wire rack. Cut into wedges to serve. Serve warm or at room temperature.

Makes 8 servings

FOURTH OF JULY PHYLLO CUPS

The pretty colors make this truly a work of art! Use strawberries or raspberries to top this special treat.

8 oz. cream cheese, softened
½ cup powdered sugar
grated peel and juice of 1 lemon
48 phyllo cups, page 8
1 cup fresh strawberries or raspberries
1 cup fresh blueberries

With a food processor or electric mixer, combine cream cheese, powdered sugar, lemon juice and grated peel until light. Spoon into prepared phyllo cups. Quarter strawberries lengthwise or use whole raspberries. Top each filled cup with a strawberry piece or raspberry. Add a few blueberries to each. Serve immediately.

Makes 48

PHYLLO CUPS WITH GRAND MARNIER CREAM CHEESE

These make a delightful dessert after a heavy holiday meal. Do not assemble them very much in advance or the phyllo will become soggy. If you don't wish to use Grand Marnier, substitute orange marmalade.

48 phyllo cups, page 8
8 oz. cream cheese, softened
½ cup powdered sugar
3 tbs. Grand Marnier liqueur

1 can (16 oz.) whole berry cranberry sauce
2 tbs. finely chopped almonds, optional

Combine cream cheese and powdered sugar with a food processor or an electric mixer. When fluffy, add Grand Marnier. Cover and chill until use. To fill phyllo cups, use a small teaspoon to place filling in prepared cup. Top with a spoonful of cranberries and sprinkle with finely chopped almonds, if desired. Serve immediately. If cranberry sauce is left, save for another use.

Makes 48

POACHED PEARS BAKED IN PHYLLO

This recipe may seem complicated, but take it one step at a time
—you will have an extraordinary dessert which will impress your
guests on a cozy winter evening. Bosc pears are best, but Anjou
or Comice work well. If you don't care for blue cheese, they are
also good without the filling.

4 firm but ripe pears, with stems
3 cups water
½ cup white wine
⅓ cup sugar
1 stick cinnamon
2 whole cloves
3 oz. cream cheese, softened
3 oz. blue cheese, crumbled
12 sheets phyllo
½ cup butter, melted

In a small saucepan which will hold pears upright, combine water, wine, sugar and spices. Bring to a boil, reduce heat and simmer for 10 minutes. Prepare pears. Cut a slice off the bottom so they will sit flat. Place in pan with poaching liquid and simmer to tender when pierced by a sharp knife, about 10 minutes. Cool completely. Remove cores from the bottom using a sharp knife or a melon baller. Combine cream cheese and blue cheese in a small bowl. Fill pears with cheese mixture.

On a work surface, brush a sheet of phyllo with butter; repeat twice. Place a filled pear in the center, gather phyllo up around top of pear and allow excess to fold back. Trim excess to 2 inches using scissors. Discard trimmings. Brush outside with butter. Repeat with remaining 3 pears. Heat oven to 400°. Place pears on a rimmed baking sheet and bake for 20 minutes or until golden. Cool for 10 minutes. Serve on dessert plates with a knife and dessert fork.

Makes 4 servings

APPLE STRUDEL

It"s easy to chop nuts and slice apples with a food processor.

½ cup finely ground almonds
   or walnuts
½ cup sugar
½ tsp. nutmeg
½ tsp. cinnamon
½ cup fine dry breadcrumbs
6 tart apples, peeled and cored
½ cup sugar
¼ cup brown sugar

½ cup raisins
2 tbs. flour
¼ tsp. salt
¼ tsp. cinnamon
¼ tsp. nutmeg
¼ tsp. grated lemon peel
phyllo and melted butter for
   strudel, page 5
confectioners' sugar

Preheat oven to 375°. In a food processor or a blender, process nuts with sugar, nutmeg and cinnamon. Place in a small bowl, add breadcrumbs and set aside. Slice apples. Combine apples, sugars, raisins, flour, spices and lemon peel. Mix well.

Fill according to strudel instructions. Bake for 1 hour or until golden and apples are tender. Dust the top with confectioners' sugar and cut into slices to serve. Serve warm.

Makes 8 servings

CHERRY CREAM CHEESE STRUDEL

*Creamy cheese and tart cherries make this ideal
for enjoying with a cup of tea.*

11 oz. cream cheese, softened
½ cup sugar
2 egg yolks
1 tsp. cinnamon
1 can (16 oz.) tart pie cherries, well drained
phyllo and melted butter for strudel, page 5
extra granulated sugar for phyllo layers

With a food processor or electric mixer, combine cream cheese, sugar, egg yolks and cinnamon until fluffy. Fold in cherries. Follow strudel shaping instructions, sprinkling each phyllo sheet with about 1 tbs. sugar as you layer. Bake at 375° for 25 to 35 minutes.

Makes 8 servings

CREAM CHEESE AND RAISIN STRUDEL

This old-fashioned filling evokes memories of days gone by. It really helps to soak raisins in very hot water before using them, to plump them up and make them softer. Another hint: Rinse walnuts in a sieve before using. You will be amazed at how much of the papery skin rinses away. Shake the water off and toast the walnuts at 350° for 10 minutes before proceeding.

¼ cup butter, softened
¼ cup sugar
2 egg yolks
11 oz. cream cheese, softened
½ cup whipping cream

1 tsp. grated lemon peel
½ cup raisins
½ cup chopped walnuts
phyllo and melted butter for
   strudel, page 5

With a food processor or electric mixer, combine butter, sugar and egg yolks until light. Add cream cheese, whipping cream and lemon peel. Mix until well blended. Stir in raisins and walnuts with a spoon. Make strudel according to shaping instructions.

Makes 8 servings

CHOCOLATE MOUSSE IN A PHYLLO CRUST

*You can use any liqueur you like to flavor this rich mousse –
Bailey's Irish Cream, Grand Marnier, amaretto or Kahlua.*

8 oz. semisweet chocolate
1 tbs. instant coffee granules
5 tbs. water
5 eggs, separated
2 tbs. rum or other liqueur

1 phyllo crust, bottom only,
  page 9
1 cup whipping cream, whipped
2 tbs. powdered sugar
1 tsp. vanilla extract

Melt chocolate in the microwave or in a double boiler. Dissolve coffee in water. Cool chocolate to room temperature. Add coffee mixture and egg yolks. Whip egg whites until stiff and fold in. Chill. Just before serving, spoon mousse into prepared phyllo crust. Whip cream with powdered sugar and vanilla. Top with whipped cream and cut into wedges to serve.

Makes 8 servings

INDEX